Education
Shire
Shin
Reading
RG2 9XD

KU-765-855

Making a Nest

Paul Bennett

Wayland

Nature's Secrets

Catching a Meal
Changing Shape
Hibernation
Making a Nest
Migration
Pollinating a Flower

Cover: A male red-headed weaver bird builds its intricate nest.
Title page: A green-throated carib hummingbird sits on her tiny nest.
Contents page: A chimpanzee builds a nest to sleep in high up in the trees.

Series editor: Francesca Motisi
Editors: Joan Walters and Francesca Motisi
Series designer: Joyce Chester
Consultant: Stephen Savage

First published in 1994 by
Wayland (Publishers) Ltd
61 Western Road, Hove
East Sussex BN3 1JD, England

© Copyright 1994 Wayland (Publishers) Limited

British Library Cataloguing in Publication Data

Bennett, Paul
    Making a Nest. - (Nature's Secrets)
    Series)
    I. Title II. Series
    591.56

ISBN 0-7502-1060-5

Printed and bound in Italy by
G. Canale & C.S.p.A., Turin

Picture acknowledgements
The publishers would like to thank the following for allowing their photographs to be reproduced in this book: Bruce Coleman Ltd 4 (top/M. P. L. Fogden), 6 (Jeremy Grayson), 7 (main/Pekka Helo), 10 (below/W. S. Paton), 11 (Konrad Wothe), 17 (main/Kim Taylor), 18 (top/Adrian Davies), 20 (J. Foott), 21 (main/Adrian Davies), 23 (main/R. I. M. Campbell, inset and contents page/Dieter & Mary Plage), 24 (Kim Taylor), 25 (Jane Burton), 26 (C. B. & D. W. Frith), 27 (Bruce Coleman Ltd), 28 (main/Frans Lanting, inset/David Hughes), 29 (Carol Hughes); Frank Lane Picture Agency 10 (above/John Hawkins), 14 (Martin B. Withers), 22 (A. Wharton); Natural History Photographic Agency cover (Peter Johnson), 5 (top/Stephen Dalton), 8 & 9 (Nigel Dennis), 12 (top/Melvin Grey, bottom/Nigel Dennis), 18 (bottom/Anthony Bannister), 19 (inset/S. Robinson); Oxford Scientific Films 4 (bottom/Dan Guravitch), 5 (bottom/Owen Newman), 7 (inset & title page/Robert A. Tyrrell), 13 (main/Doug Allan, inset/Roland Mayr), 15 (top/Stephen Mills), 16 Bob Goodale, 17 (inset/Colin Milkins), 19 (main/John Cooke), 21 (inset/G. I. Bernard); Papilio 15 (bottom/BIRDSRKP).

Contents

What is a nest?   4

Bird nests   6

Mini-beast nests   16

Nest-making mammals   20

Fish nests   24

Reptile nests   26

Glossary   30

Books to read   31

Notes for parents and teachers   31

Index   32

What is a nest?

A nest is a place where eggs are laid and hatched. It can also be a place where young animals are born and looked after until they are big enough to leave the nest. Some animals use nests as a place to rest and sleep.

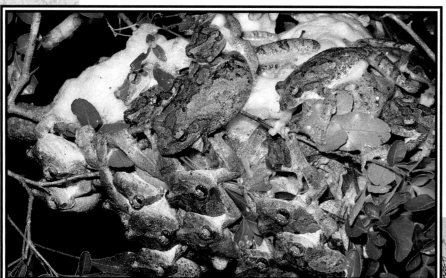

◁ Grey tree frogs lay their spawn in a frothy white nest. Later the tadpoles will hatch and drop into the water.

△ In very bad weather polar bears may dig day-beds in a snowdrift. They use a different den for their cubs.

Some nests have many creatures of the same species living in them. This bee's nest hums with activity. ▷

Helpless dormouse babies sleep safely in their nest. Dormice make one nest to sleep in during the day and another for hibernating in during the winter. Before she gives birth, the mother makes a third nest for her young. ▽

Bird nests

Birds build all kinds of nests. Some are simple hollows in the ground. Others are fancy frameworks hanging from tree branches.

△ Most birds build bowl-shaped nests from twigs, grass, leaves or mud. This blackbird has chosen to build its nest on the ground, which is unusual. Blackbirds usually build their nests in trees where their eggs and chicks will be safe from predators.

Ospreys ▷
make massive
and untidy
nests of sticks
and twigs.
Their nests can
be as tall as a
fully grown
human.

◁ A green-
throated carib
hummingbird
sits on her tiny
nest – it's only
the size of a two
pence piece!

In Africa the thick-billed weaver bird twists grass together to make its nest.

House martins
build their nests
on the walls of
buildings from
the blobs of mud
they gather.

A flamingo's
muddy
mound has a
neat, saucer-
shaped top
for the egg
to sit in.

The colourful kingfisher tunnels into the soft soil or sand of a river bank to make a nest. At the end of the tunnel is a chamber where the eggs are laid. ▷

Here is a colony of dazzling carmine bee-eaters. ▽

△ The jackass penguins
of Argentina burrow
into the soil to make
their nests.

Woodpeckers make a
nest in a hole
in a tree. ▷

The cuckoo doesn't make its own nest –
instead it lays its eggs in other birds'
nests. As soon as the cuckoo egg
hatches it pushes out all the other
young birds and eggs from the nest.
This poor sedge warbler is worn
out trying to feed this monstrous
cuckoo chick.

Don't wobble the branch!
A white tern has
balanced its egg in a
small hollow on a tree
branch. ▷

Look carefully to find a
plover's eggs on this
pebble beach. They are
camouflaged by the
smooth, round stones. ▽

Mini-beast nests

Mini-beasts build a wide range of nests.
Some are very simple, such as the
burrow made by the solitary wasp.
Others are very large and made up of
many parts, such as the termite's nest.

△ Termites build their mounds from
tiny particles of earth. The nest starts
underground and is built by worker
termites. Some mounds are huge and
even taller than a bus.

These black ants have dug out networks of underground tunnels. There are 'rooms' for storing food and for looking after the eggs, grubs and cocoons. ▷

Wood ants build their nests in forests. They look like a neat pile of twigs and inside there may be as many as 100,000 ants. ▽

△ The queen wasp busily builds her nest around the small comb that holds her tiny eggs. The worker wasps that she produces continue to build the nest.

◁ These are paper wasps – their nest looks very papery. You can see the white grubs in the comb's delicate cells.

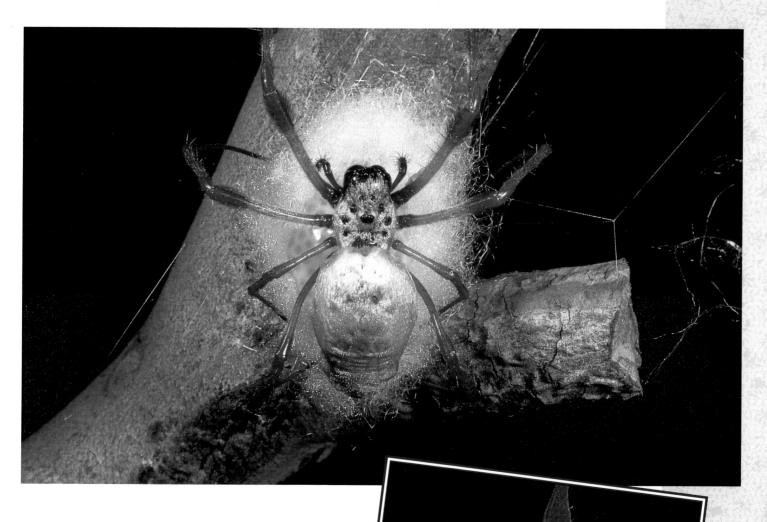

△ Large, small or 'hairy' spiders of all types build a kind of nest for their eggs. In Australia, an orb-weaving spider lays her eggs on a soft cushion of silk that she has spun.

A sac spider looks menacing as she guards her nest that she has spun between two leaves. ▷

Nest-making mammals

Mammals are animals whose females give birth to live young which they feed with milk from their bodies. Many different mammals make nests where they can rest, breed and feed their young.

△ Shhh!
In California, USA, a kangaroo rat is fast asleep in its desert burrow. It has lined its nest with grass.

Squirrels build two nests called dreys – one for the summer and one for the winter. ▷

The mole's spade-like feet make it a
good digger. It lives underground where
it makes its nest and comes to the
surface to push out the unwanted soil.
The mound of soil is called a molehill.

A chimpanzee builds a nest to sleep in at night. It is bending branches across to make a platform high up in the trees. ▷

Heavy adult gorillas would crash through the branches if they tried to nest high up in the trees. Instead, they make a nest from branches and leaves on the ground. ▽

Fish nests

A male and female fish will come together in the same area of water, and lay and fertilize their eggs. Some fish like to build a nest for the eggs where they will have a good chance of survival.

△ The colourful male stickleback drives the plain female from his nest after she has laid her eggs. The nest is made from pieces of water plants.

The splendid male Siamese fighting fish makes a layer of bubbles on the surface of the water.

After fertilizing the eggs he spits them into his nest of bubbles!

Reptile nests

Many reptiles, such as alligators, crocodiles and turtles, make nests for their eggs.

△ This female crocodile is building her nest by using her powerful back legs.

The female alligator lays her eggs in an
untidy mound of mud and rotting
vegetation. She will guard her nest
until the eggs hatch, about two to three
months later. When she hears the
babies 'peeping' inside, she removes
the vegetation carefully to help
them escape.

A ridley's turtle digs a nest in the sand with her flippers. ▽

She lays her eggs in a pit that she has scooped out and which she will fill in before returning to the sea. ▷

About two months later, the baby turtles hatch from their eggs. Then they scramble out of the nest and down to the sea where they will be safe from birds that like to eat them. ▽

Glossary

Camouflaged Disguised so that it is not easily seen against its background.

Cells The small compartments or 'rooms' that make up the nests of bees and wasps.

Chamber A 'room' or place in a nest where an animal can rest or sleep.

Colony A group of animals of the same type living together.

Drey The nest of squirrels.

Comb A collection of cells made by bees and wasps.

Fertilize To bring together a female cell or egg and a male cell or sperm so that an animal will produce young.

Grubs The form of an insect that hatches from an egg. The correct name for a grub is a larva.

Hibernating Resting during the winter months.

Particles Very small pieces.

Predators Animals that hunt and kill other animals for food.

Reptile An animal, such as a lizard, snake, or turtle, which has a backbone, a scaly skin, and is cold-blooded and usually fully adapted to living on land.

Spawn A mass of eggs from a frog or a fish.

Species A group of animals or plants that are alike in most ways.

Vegetation Plant life.

Books to read

Amazing Animal Babies, Christopher Maynard (Dorling Kindersley, 1993)

Animal Parents, Tony Seddon (Hodder and Stoughton, 1989)

Bird, David Burnie (Dorling Kindersley, 1990)

Insect, Laurence Mound (Dorling Kindersley, 1990)

Mammal, Steve Parker (Dorling Kindersley, 1989)

Reptiles, Philip Steele (Macmillan Publishers Ltd., 1990)

The Life Cycle of a Stickleback, Philip Parker (Wayland Publishers Ltd., 1988)

Discovering Nature (Wayland Publishers Ltd), a series of books that takes a wide look at animals and plants.

Notes for parents and teachers

Project: **Birds' Nests**

Birds will often nest in and around your garden. You can find out what nesting materials different types of bird prefer. Put a selection of materials in your garden; such as dead grasses, moss, twigs, leaves, pieces of string and pieces of paper. Keep watch to see what materials the different birds like best. Keep a diary of your observations.

Have a look around the area where you live to see what other bird nests you can find. Some birds nest in trees, below the eaves of houses or near ponds and rivers. Always watch from a safe distance or you will frighten the birds away. Make a note of any discoveries in your diary.

Project: **Fishes' Nests**

You can set up an aquarium to watch a male three-spined stickleback make his nest. Cover the bottom of the aquarium with a layer of gravel and a few rocks. Fill the aquarium with water. Pond or rain water is best. If using tap water, allow it to stand for forty-eight hours to allow the chlorine to escape. Some three-spined sticklebacks live in salt or brackish water and so this water will need to be used instead of fresh water.

The male will collect pieces of pond plant to make his nest. Catch one or two female sticklebacks and place them in the tank. If you are lucky the fish will breed and lay eggs. The adult sticklebacks can be fed fish food, live daphnia (water fleas) and similar. Any young fish that hatch can be fed on a liquid fish food for young fry. This can be purchased from an aquarium or pet shop. Keep a diary of your observations.

Places to visit: You may see other animal nests mentioned in this book while visiting a zoo, aquarium or nature park.

Index

alligator 26, 27
ants 17
Australia 19

bees 5
birds 6, 7, 8, 9, 10,
    11, 12, 13, 14,
    15
  blackbird 6
  carib 7
  carmine bee-
    eaters 12
  flamingo 11
  house martin 10
  jackass
    penguins 13
  kingfisher 12
  osprey 7
  plover 15
  weaver 8–9
  white tern 15
  woodpecker 13

camouflage 15
chimpanzee 23
crocodile 26

dormouse 5

dreys 20, 21

eggs 4, 6, 11, 12,
    14, 15, 17, 18,
    19, 24, 25, 26,
    27, 28

fish 24–25
  Siamese
    fighting 25
  stickleback 24

gorillas 23

kangaroo rat 20

mammals 20–23
mole 22
mud nests 11–12

nests
  bubbles 25
  burrows 13, 16
  earth 16
  grass 6, 8–9, 20
  leaves 6, 20, 23
  mud 6, 10, 11,
    27

sand 28
snow 4
trees 13, 23
tunnels 12, 17,
    22
twigs 6, 7, 17,
    20
water plants 24

polar bears 4

reptiles 26–29
  alligators 26, 27
  crocodiles 26
  turtles 26,
    28–29

spiders 19
squirrels 20, 21

tadpoles 4
termites 16
tree frogs 4
turtles 26, 28–29

USA 20

wasps 16, 18